This Journal Belongs to :

Made in United States
Troutdale, OR
10/27/2023

14027878R00060